A Photo for Fred

by Marilee Robin Burton
illustrated by Meryl Henderson

Practice Decodable 70

Mc Graw Hill Education

Bothell, WA • Chicago, IL • Columbus, OH • New York, NY

MHEonline.com

Send all inquiries to:
McGraw-Hill Education
8787 Orion Place
Columbus, OH 43240

ISBN: 978-0-02-130451-6
MHID: 0-02-130451-3

Printed in China.

8 9 10 11 12 DSS 27 26 25 24 23

Phil got a puppy named Ralph. Phil wanted to send a photo to his pal Fred.

Phil and Ralph went to a photo shop.
Ralph just ran and ran.

Ralph's photo was a blur.

"Ralph!" muttered Phil. "You look like a funny pheasant!"

"I will take his photo myself!" said Phil. Ralph did not sit still.

"Ralph!" grumbled Phil. "How can I get a photo if you don't stay still?"

Phil phoned Fred and said, "Come over.
I have a surprise to show you!"